Now that you're a manager, do you know what to do?

Let this book be your guide. You'll learn how to:

- Create a positive work environment.
- Define and understand the culture of your organization.
- Understand the effectiveness of "management by wandering around."
- Find your leaders and set them free.
- Negotiate from principles, issues, and values.
- Practice leadership.
- Encourage the best in people.
- Manage the inevitable crisis.
- Bring your compassion to the workplace.
- Unleash human spirit and creativity.
- Be brave.

Here's help for the road ahead.

"I just finished reading Rod Collins' *What Do I Do When I Get There?* My only question is this: Where was this book thirty years ago on my first day of my first management job? Buy it. Read it. You'll love it. Come to think of it, buy two. You'll need a backup when you wear it out."

Alex Lafollette, Restaurant Manager
and author of *The Camas Place*

"*What Do I Do When I Get There?* is the day-to-day reality of management. Forged from years of tough, pragmatic and innovative problem solving, Rod Collins divulges his simple formulas for business success that every manager in the real world must learn to master."

Bill DeLaney, Director of Management Studies
USDA Forest Service (Retired)

"My guys loved it! We are a totally decentralized team, and I'm using the chapters, one at a time, as a monthly feature for our status conference calls. The topics of the chapters have added an excellent opportunity to enhance our leadership development."

Ron Karsten, Manager, Field Operations
Electric Lightwave, LLC

"I think a new manager can take this book and just open it every morning and decide what to do, right down to relationships with subordinate staff."

J.C. Hansen, Director of Administration
for Rural Development, State of Hawaii, USDA

What Do I Do When I Get There?

What Do I Do When I Get There?
A New Manager's Guidebook

Rod Collins

Bright Works Press
Springfield, Oregon

2007
Bright Works Press
Springfield, OR

Copyright © Rodney D. Collins 2007

All rights reserved. No part of this book may be reproduced, stored in a retrieval system, or transmitted in any form or by any means, electronic, mechanical, photocopying, recording, or otherwise, without the written permission of the author.

Printed in the United States of America

CIP Data
Collins, Rodney D., 1941-
 What Do I Do When I Get There?
 A New Manager's Guidebook
 p. cm
 LCCN 2006901677

  ISBN: 0-9778805-0-8
  ISBN: 978-0-9778805-0-8

  1. Management. I. Title
  HD31.C6138 2006   658
         QB106-600118

Cover Design & Illustrations by Julia O'Reilly, www.juliaoreilly.com

Back Cover Photo by David Simone, www.davidsimone.com

Editing & Book Design by Eva Long

The Life Cycle of Organizations *illustration on page 31 was conceived by Harrison Owen and is illustrated and published here with his permission.*

---

for Vi

Contents

INTRODUCTION — 3

1 FIRST DAYS:
Walk, Look, & Listen — 11

2 LEADERSHIP:
It's All Around You — 23

3 RULES & REGS:
Weed Your Bureaucratic Garden — 29

4 BUILDING YOUR TEAM:
The Power of Acknowledgment — 37

5 THE POWER OF THANK YOU:
Positive Reinforcement & Recognition — 45

6 ENCOURAGE PARTICIPATION:
Blow the Lid Off That Suggestion Box   55

7 SMOKE & MIRRORS:
The Line-Item Budget   61

8 THE DIFFICULT TASK OF FIRING:
With Humanity & Justice For All   71

9 VALUES-BASED NEGOTIATION:
Bargaining Is No Bargain   81

10 A READING LIST:
Beyond the Simple Guide   91

11 CHAPTER SUMMARIES:
The Shortcut   99

ACKNOWLEDGMENTS   104

Introduction

Introduction

The new manager is still left with the choice to either "act the part" or to imitate someone else.

I became a manager just like you did.

I started at the beginning.

My first real job was working in a small grocery store in the little town of Shady Cove, Oregon, in the north end of the Rogue River Valley. I was 14 years old, growing up in a logging and milling town. Although my grocery store job didn't have the macho status of bucking hay bales for local farmers, I was taught a number of valuable lessons by Wally Crank, proprietor of the Shady Cove Market.

The first thing Wally did was train me. He taught me can sizes, how to stock shelves, how to track inventory, how to organize the back of the store so the most popular items were easy to find for quick replacement on the shelves, how to price items based on wholesale costs, how to arrange the produce counters, and how to deal with customers, especially the crabby ones.

The second thing Wally did was trust me to do my job. If I fouled up something, Wally let me know about it, trained me again, and then turned me loose to do my job.

I earned $596 that summer.

My next real job was working in an auto-wrecking yard for a hard taskmaster—my father, John Collins. The scenario was much the same as at Wally's place. My dad trained me, corrected my mistakes, and trusted me to do the job.

At 16, I was driving a tow truck, picking up damaged vehicles—salvage—and my dad trusted my judgment and skill. This was another growing season for me. I earned enough to buy my first car, a 1950 Ford sedan.

Over the years, I worked jobs as a farmhand, operated a backhoe and drove a dump truck, sewed sacks in a grain cleaner, and drove a school bus.

To pay my way through college, I worked summers as a firefighter for the U.S. Forest Service on the Fremont National Forest in Lakeview, Oregon. I always liked the woods, and the summers on the Fremont just hooked me.

I managed the paperback section of the college bookstore—and doubled gross sales in one year—edited the college newspaper, worked as a writer-editor for the Oregon Department of Education, and pumped gas and serviced vehicles.

The common themes in all those jobs were the same. There were mechanical and technical tasks to be done, things to learn, clean and clear steps to follow, measurable results by which to judge success. And that was where it stopped.

INTRODUCTION

Looking back over a multitude of jobs I've held, the only other people who took the time to actually train me for the job I was hired to do were Maurice Dodson, owner of Maurice Dodson's Union 76 service station, and the guys on the Fremont.

When I got the job of editor for my small college newspaper, I was suddenly a manager. But since the only examples I had of being a manager were Wally, Dad, and Maurice, I did what a lot of first-time managers and supervisors do: I faked it.

At age 24, I received my teaching credential, and the first time I stepped into a high school classroom as a freshly-laundered English teacher in Hubbard, Oregon, I was terrified someone would discover I didn't know what I was doing. Certainly nothing in my college education prepared me for anything more complicated than making out lesson plans and talking in front of people without falling down from fright.

Thanks to Arlie Holt, a good master teacher who suffered me through my student teaching, I could act like I knew what I was doing. By the end of my second year, I began to think I actually knew something.

The first time I supervised another human being, the experience was much the same, except that I didn't have anyone called a "master supervisor" to help me. I started off acting the part, and eventually ended up with some knowledge and understanding of my position.

Missing life in the woods, I left my career as a starving teacher some years later, and jumped at the chance to go to work for the Forest Service again. This led to a position as the personnel officer on the Fremont National Forest. I did a much better job at covering my deficiencies because I had taken away some knowledge and wisdom from all the jobs I'd held before this one. Some say I did a good job in personnel, but again, the first year was one of terror. I knew—just knew—that someone would discover that I was making it all up.

Moving along in my career, as administrative officer on the Ochoco National Forest in Prineville, Oregon, I was asked to lead a pilot program to test how efficiently a National Forest could operate if unnecessary budget restrictions were lifted. Productivity improved 25% the first year of this new program, and 35% by the end of the second year. I learned some important principles about the good, the bad, and the ugly of the lump-sum budgeting model vs. the line-item budget allocation model. (You'll find these in Chapter 7.)

Along the way in the Forest Service, I received the Secretary of Agriculture's Award; a Chief's Award; and the Chief's Medal of Excellence, the only one ever given by the Forest Service.

I retired from the Forest Service in 1999.

In 1993, I was proud to be chosen to serve on Vice President Gore's National Performance Review, an effort to reinvent government. Those months spent in Washington, D.C. were rewarding, but I always kept the nose of my vehicle pointed west.

INTRODUCTION

When it comes to technical tasks, we know to train people. When it comes to so-called softer subjects like supervision and mentoring, we haven't progressed much at all, and the new manager is still left with the choice to "act the part" or imitate someone else. Either path is strewn with banana peels.

Current management literature is full of good advice:

- Know your company's business.
- Know what you do best.
- Create your vision.
- Lead by example.
- Empower employees.
- Be honest.
- Thrive on chaos.
- Think globally, act locally.

All good stuff.

Then there are endless materials about roles and responsibilities. They usually begin, "The Manager of X is responsible for overseeing the budget and the financial execution of Y Company, for supervising the sales force, and for leading the Quality Team."

But there is little discussion of the nuts and bolts actions of the good manager. "What do I do?" "What do I say?" "How do I behave?" "Who do I talk to?" "How shall I talk to them?" These answers are missing from most of our training.

So we new managers make it up as we go. Or we imitate the behavior of successful managers we know and try to be someone else. These don't work for the long term.

After years of working jobs where I faked it until I learned the nuts and bolts of management leadership, and after looking over the abundance of management books, I concluded that what was needed was a simple guide to help the new manager get through the first few months.

My experience tells me that successful managers teach themselves by trial and error. Good managers have good instincts and from experience, they'll extract a few principles they can use repetitively.

Then they write books.

If this simple guide helps you make fewer errors in those trials ahead and cultivates your own instincts as well, I'll be delighted.

Rod Collins
rod@brightworkspress.com
www.brightworkspress.com

1
FIRSTDAYS:
Walk, Look, & Listen

1
FIRST DAYS: Walk, Look, & Listen

---

*There is no Hippocratic Oath for new managers,
but there ought to be, and it should read:
First, Do No Harm.*

I remember seeing the newly-promoted CEO, formerly the parts manager of a large truck dealership, sweeping the walk in front of his business each morning, and I wondered if he would ever make the transition from "doer" to manager. He never did, and the dealership soon went out of business. I never talked to him after the business closed, so I can only guess at the psychology behind his actions. He had been promoted for hard work—for doing stuff—and I suspect he always felt uncomfortable when he wasn't physically working. The tragedy is that he also put a large number of people out of work for a time, including some of his suppliers.

When you move up the corporate ladder to become a manager, it's because you've proven yourself an exceptional engineer, or buyer, machinist, analyst, forester, designer, marketing rep, or software programmer.

As a new manager, however, the first thing you must understand is that you're no longer responsible to produce your product; you have a new role now. In smaller companies and organizations, you may need to do some hands-on work, but to paraphrase author and management guru Tom Peters, you have given up honest work for good.

In simple terms, your new responsibility is to create a positive, productive work environment. If that sounds a bit vague, it is, but when you see a highly charged, turned-on work force, you'll recognize it. Positive, productive work environments don't always mean nice offices, liberal amounts of workspace, and benefits packages. Those may be the by-products of a highly motivated work force, but they seldom create it. Some of the most highly charged work forces in the world are the Incident Management Teams that fight our larger wildfires. That work environment is as adverse as it gets.

> **Your new responsibility is to create a positive, productive work environment.**

In talking with other managers over the years, our collective wisdom led us to the conclusion that we had about three weeks to establish our credibility as a manager. We all agreed that we each felt a certain amount of fear that someone would discover we were imposters much sooner than that. You'll need to have patience with yourself and good listening skills with others in these first days. But **First, Do No Harm.**

If you've been promoted from the ranks, then you already know some of what you need to know. You already understand the culture of the organization, you probably know those people who can get things done, you probably already know "the gatekeepers"—those operational power brokers who can make or break a proposal—as well as the naysayers, the disaffected, and the winners.

However, if you're from outside the organization, or even if you've changed offices within the company, you're starting from scratch.

First Days

Whether promoted in-house, or you're the new kid in town, here's how to get your legs under you these first few days:

Get Out of Your Office

Before you call any meeting, get out of your office. Practice what Tom Peters calls "Management By Wandering Around." Nothing signals your interest in the work force and the business of the company better than a casual visit from the boss. It can be as simple as getting your coffee cup and wandering the hallways, talking with people, asking what they're working on.

Read Everything You Can About the Company

Be the best-informed newcomer on the block. Don't grouse about E-mail. Read it. It will contain tidbits that are useful in building your big picture of the company, and it will certainly give you strong signals about the culture and values of the company.

Don't Be in a Hurry to Make Changes

Every new manager creates an opportunity for people to dust off old skeletons and "rattle them bones" one more time. It may take the form of past grievances, or it may take the form of a really good idea that hasn't been accepted yet. Listen and evaluate, but don't be hasty—not in these first days.

Get Acquainted With Your Peers

They'll know the ropes and, if you're lucky, at least one will be a mentor. Even here, it's wise to go slowly. Be aware that some of your peers' efforts at mentoring, however well meaning, could be intended to create divisive alliances as opposed to true mentoring.

Get Acquainted With Your Boss

Of all my bosses, only one, Forest Supervisor Bill McCleese, ever took the time to help me get oriented. Bill spent the first week with me. He created some starter tasks for me, took me to the outlying ranger districts, stood me up beside him and announced, "This is Rod. He is my administrative officer." It was powerful stuff and in retrospect, I think he knew I'd be winging it during my first year. He knew I had a steep learning curve ahead of me.

Get Acquainted With the Assistant

In some companies, your boss may be unavailable most of the time. Persist anyway in getting at least a few minutes time each week. If your boss has an assistant, get to know him or her. Leave notes about what you're doing, and ask the assistant to set up a time for you to meet with your boss. Follow up to make sure your notes are actually delivered.

DELIVER BAD NEWS IN PERSON

Always deliver bad news in person and be the first to deliver it, because every company has at least one "spin doctor" who always seems to have it wrong. When it comes to bad news, get to your boss first with it. Be factual. Be brave.

Your Organization's Culture

There may be company manuals, vision statements, employee handbooks, union contracts and the like available to you. Read those, but pay closer attention to the war stories that circulate through the hallways or on the company grapevine.

It's an odd quirk of human nature, but good listeners always give the impression of having shared a great deal even when they haven't said a word.

A side benefit may be your awareness of how closely the culture of the company reflects the CEO's stated values. If the culture parallels those values, you're probably in a pretty good place.

If you've been listening to your peers and to your staff, you're starting to identify your internal customers—the "purchasers" of the services you as a manager provide to the other employees. It's useful to keep a list of your internal customers, complete with the details you will learn by walking around. These details will help you serve your internal customers better. Don't expect to remember everything. Write it down. Be specific. Keep it private.

If your predecessor left you any personal files, dust those off and read them. Here again, you can learn something about the culture of the company. Anticipate that you'll find things not completed by your predecessor. These may be key to your first actions as a new manager.

So now you're getting a feel for the culture of the company. You walk the hallways at least once a day and stop in on your work group to chat, to get a feel for how the group is doing. You have at least one peer to talk to. You've become acquainted with your boss. You've read all you can about the company. You've listened to the stories people have brought your way. If there are off-site facilities, you've visited all of them. You've signed a few memos. You're establishing relationships with both your internal and external clients. You're starting to become a fixture within the company.

> **The true culture of an organization is passed on through the stories the employees tell you.**

Calling The First Meeting

If the demands of your new job allow it, give yourself a month to six weeks of just doing the routine work. Then when it feels right, it's time for a formal meeting with your subordinates.

FIRST DAYS

The first meeting is critical, so take the time to prepare a complete agenda, even if you supervise only a few people. Believe that you are about to sell your first product—your service and support of your work group.

The first people I supervised were personnel specialists, six in all. For the first meeting I called, I wrote the agenda as though I was to address a multitude.

First, I wanted them to know I valued honesty. If they had good news, I wanted to share in that. If the news was bad, that was perhaps more important because it might signal a need for improvements in the operation. If they were successful, I'd let the world know about it. If there was a problem, I'd take the heat.

Second, I gave them my first impressions of their competence. Fortunately it was positive, and I was grateful for their competence and diligence, which had given me time to observe and study. (If your first impressions are less than complimentary, see Chapter 4.)

Third, we talked about customers, and we set customer service goals. Note I said "*we* set customer service goals." Two dynamics are at work here. One is that all employees want to succeed in their jobs. The other is that employees are world experts at their jobs. No one else knows as much about their jobs as they do. Seasoned employees understand the internal processes, the volume of the work, the seasonal peaks, the training required to do the work effectively, whom to get help from in tough situations, etc.

The first meeting is critical, so take the time to prepare a complete agenda.

Fourth, we wrote a plan for the following six months, complete with training needs, equipment needs, personal contact needs, and customer service goals. We also developed a customer feedback process to track our effectiveness. Our feedback process was crude, but at least our thinking was right in understanding the need for the process and the need to create it.

> **I wanted them to know I depended on them.**

Finally, I wanted them to know I depended on them to bring their adult minds to the job. To underscore my point, I delegated responsibility for routine personnel actions to a woman on my staff and grandly titled her position "Supervisory Personnel Management Specialist." Via memo to the rest of the organization, I formally appointed her as the acting personnel officer with full authority to make decisions and take action during my absences.

Building Trust

Employees will generally take you at face value, so it's important to keep your word. When the news was good and I wanted to tell the executive team, the information was often presented to the executive team by someone from my staff. Give credit where credit is deserved. When the news was bad, I delivered it myself to the executive team. These moments call for your leadership.

Establishing your reputation for honesty and courage is important. At the very least, your integrity and reputation will give you freedom to innovate, access to power, and a degree of forgiveness if you make a mistake.

The First Crisis

All of these steps presume you are in a stable company, with a stable work force, clear goals, and routine processes. But what will you do during your first days if a crisis develops? (And it will.) If circumstances force you into a decision for which you have inadequate information, don't hurry it. Gather as much intelligence as you can, pick the best brains you can find, choose what seems the best course of action, and then sleep on it. Late afternoon or nighttime plans may look good initially, but we see things differently when our minds are fresh. If you're boxed in and must decide, then do it. The sins of commission are easier to correct than the sins of omission. It's an old saw, but a true one: Failure to reach a decision is a decision.

Setting Boundaries

As people begin to trust you, they'll bring you their personal problems. If it's job related, it's your duty to be a responsible counselor and advisor. If it's about personal matters, don't play amateur psychologist or rescuer. Serious personal problems belong to the experts who are hired through your Employee Assistance Program. If you have a human resources office, make an appointment for your team member, and let the HR office set up the contacts for counseling. Under no circumstance assume the role of rescuer.

Keep all conversations confidential.

One last thing a new manager should keep in mind: You can be friendly and supportive of your subordinates, but you can't be friends, not in the sense of being schoolyard chums. You can have favorites among your subordinates, but you can't show it. You can socialize at company picnics and you can host business luncheons for your staff, but make sure these include all of your staff. Any action that's considered divisive sabotages your primary mission—creating a positive work environment.

2

LEADERSHIP:
It's All Around You

2
LEADERSHIP: It's All Around You

Leaders challenge the process, inspire a shared vision, enable others to act, model the way and encourage the heart.
James M. Kouzes & Barry Z. Posner, *The Leadership Challenge*

All good managers lead, and all good leaders are called upon to manage from time to time.

While it isn't worth your trouble to try to discern which management action is managing and which is leading, it is worth your time to recognize leadership when you see it. Good leadership is a worthy study.

Learn to Recognize Leadership

There seems to be a great myth that leaders occupy the top positions in an organization. This simply isn't true, and an organization that cultivates this culture is weakened because it blocks access to the skills of the work force.

What's true is that leaders are found at all levels of the organization. There are people in your organization who are leaders in fraternal organizations, youth groups, churches, Toastmasters, Rotary, 4-H, Campfire Girls, Boys and Girls Clubs.

I once managed a mid-level accountant who had the drive and skill to organize a statewide convention for 10,000 VFW members. Others I've known were active in local theater groups. Some parlayed home marketing businesses into small fortunes, some owned retail stores, a few had consulting businesses outside of the office, others taught at local colleges and served on local school boards.

> **There's a myth that leaders occupy the top positions in an organization.**

Why any organization would deny itself access to the leadership skills of these talented employees is a mystery, but many do.

The task of the new manager is to create opportunities for these leaders to bring their leadership skills to work.

This sounds easy, and, for the most part, it is. There are enough focus groups, committees, and working teams in most organizations to provide a positive outlet for your group's leaders. Harnessing this talent is a big step towards fulfilling your mission as a new manager—creating a positive work environment. Each person responsible for a work group is in a leadership position, even if it's a short-lived working team.

In a time before federal bureaucracies paid local contractors with locally written checks or credit cards, a group of purchasing agents on the Ochoco National Forest researched the laws and the administrative barriers to paying small purchases and small contracts by local check. They discovered they could piggyback on a check-writing pilot test in another Forest Service region. As their manager, I simply made one phone call to get us included in this pilot test. The leadership team had already done the legwork—they led the whole effort. All I did was endorse the project and support their energy, leadership, and success by making one short phone call.

Later, payment of small jobs by locally written checks became standard business practice for all government agencies. Because normal pay procedures could mean a delay of sixty to ninety days between delivery of service and payment for that service, some local vendors stopped working with the Forest Service. In the rural world of the Forest Service, local vendors are important, especially during wildfire emergencies.

Ask Your Employees

Another way for you to tap into the skills of your department is simply to ask the employees what they would do to improve the quality of their work, the flow of their work, service to their customers, and the quality of their personal work lives.

The answers to these will most likely fall into three categories: 1) things to stop doing, 2) things that need to be done and aren't being done, and 3) processes or products that need improving. There is a caveat, however; you may create expectations for positive change on the part of your employees that you must meet in order to maintain your personal and organizational credibility. This approach should never be undertaken lightly. (See Chapter 6.)

It always worked best for me to consult, to explain, and to request action rather than to order it. In extreme situations, such as leading fire crews, a false bomb threat or a flooding roof, there wasn't time to consult, explain, and request After the emergency was dealt with, however, there was time to critique and to refine plans for the next emergency.

> **Many people confuse power with the right to order things to happen.**

Organizations formally invest managers with a degree of power, but many people confuse power with the right to order things to happen. Sometimes that's necessary, but too much exercise of power erodes leadership. It's better to equate the power of your position with an equal degree of responsibility. Remember, the new manager's job is to create a positive work environment. Power used to that end is based on recognition of your responsibility.

3

RULES & REGS:
Weed Your Bureaucratic Garden

3
RULES & REGS: Weed Your Bureaucratic Garden

...the most abundant, least expensive, most underutilized and constantly abused resource in the world [is] human spirit and ingenuity.
Dee Huck, Founder of Visa, and the Chaordic Alliance

After thirty-plus years studying workplace psychology and how organizations succeed or fail, I'm convinced the most important ingredient in all business success or failure is human spirit. The task of the new manager is to foster a climate that encourages energy and ingenuity. How you approach your employees will depend on whether you see them as potential problems or as potential opportunities.

Let me give you an example. Through the eyes of an employee who really liked having fun at work, and who let me pick her brain, I watched a young company grow. The company's products included baseball caps with pictures or logos, foam rubber sleeves for pop cans or hot cups, coffee mugs with your "mug" on it, pennants, and tee shirts.

At the time I first became acquainted with the company, they had a loose organization of about forty people, no dress code, and everyone did whatever was needed to fill an order and get it shipped on time. Everyone worked to expand the business. Employees and managers all took breaks in the same break room. Business meetings were informal and could pretty much be called by anyone from shipping clerks to the graphic artists.

They were on a fast track. This company had cracked the Asian market and growth was exponential—every business person's dream.

The founder of this company decided to sell the business at this point, and it didn't take him very long. If you looked at the company's profit and loss statement and the incredible business growth of this company, it was a natural for someone with sufficient money to buy it.

And this is where it got interesting to me. One of the first things the new CEO did was set up reserved parking for himself and a few department heads. Then he set up an executive lunchroom separate from the employee lunchroom. Then he formalized the departments in the company, e.g., graphic arts, marketing, shipping. Finally, he instituted a dress code, clock hours, and vacation policy. Communication among specialists was minimized. As a result, unfettered human spirit and ingenuity died, and the old employees began to leave, one by one. My source, the person who really liked having fun at work, was among the first to go.

The company is still in business because they have a good product, although it isn't much larger than it was 15 years ago.

The Life Cycle of Organizations

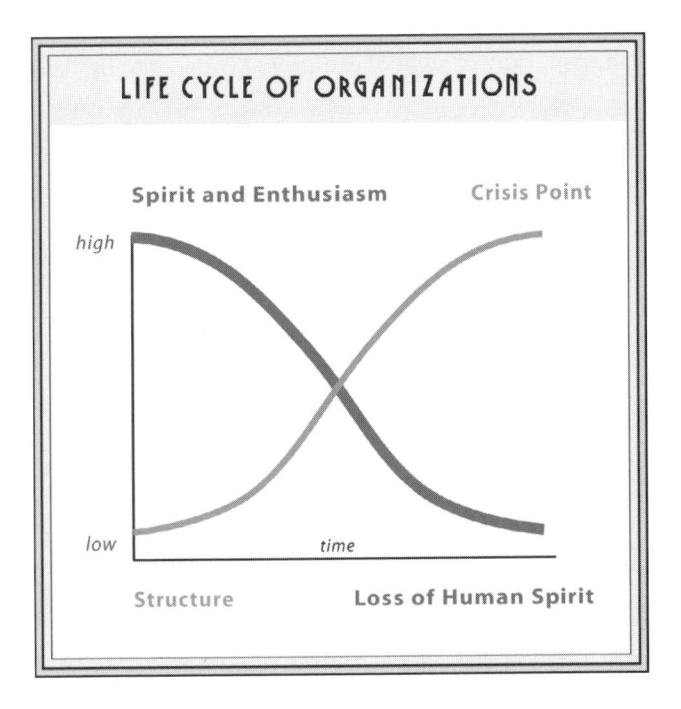

LIFE CYCLE OF ORGANIZATIONS

Spirit and Enthusiasm • Crisis Point
high / low — time
Structure • Loss of Human Spirit

This chart illustrates a typical cycle for an organization, private or public. At the beginning of any new enterprise, human spirit and creativity are high. Structure follows behind. Business processes such as checking accounts, collections, payroll, records, communications, and inventory control are all reasonable business structure to contain and support the workplace. If left unchecked, however, the structure continues to grow until it chokes the life—the human spirit, creativity and enthusiasm—out of the organization. At some point the structure becomes its own creature, a bureaucracy, and one of two things happens: either the bureaucratic garden gets weeded or the organization goes into crisis.

In the company cited above, the CEO went beyond just letting structure grow; he planted bureaucratic weeds of his own.

We can all point to personal encounters with government agencies as examples of lifeless bureaucracy. What's equally true is that private organizations follow the same path. They just don't have the luxury of tax dollars to support their ineptitude.

> **Iacocca tapped the spirit and ingenuity of his work force.**

One of the most striking examples of rigorous weeding I know is the story of Lee Iacocca's remarkable transformation of Chrysler. After borrowing some $250 million from Congress, the media carried the story that Chrysler had repaid the debt within the first year.

He simplified the company's bureaucracy. He went out on the floor of the assembly plants and asked supervisors and employees what was getting in the way of turning out a quality product the public would buy. They knew. (Remember, employees are the world's experts about their jobs.)

It sounds simplistic, but Mr. Iacocca tapped the spirit and ingenuity of his work force. He asked for their best ideas and then acted on them. He turned around a huge organization, with major help from the work force. He saved the company and repaid the Congress within a year. The complaints we have about government bureaucracies stem from the same systemic problem: unchecked structural growth—rule making.

So what does this mean for the new manager? Remember First, Do No Harm. This means creating no unnecessary rules. None. Not even apparently harmless ones. None. If you must deal with exceptions to normal operating procedures, then deal with them as exceptions. Don't create a new rule just to cover the rare or improbable "worst case" situation.

Apart from the strictures new rules place on human spirit and ingenuity, they also keep people from using their intelligence and judgment. As my budget officer, J. C. Hansen, once said, "If you write it down, people stop thinking." If you hear people saying, "That's not what the company rules say," then you know you have some weeding to do.

> **Create no unnecessary rules. None.**

My predecessor in an administrative position had a rule that his personal messages were to be left unopened, even if he was going to be gone for long periods. Those messages were generally sent in an official blue envelope. When I replaced him, I told my staff that my non-business personal messages were never sent to the office, and that my acting administrator should open the blue envelopes. If she discovered something she thought she shouldn't see, she was to put it in a new blue envelope, and seal it.

My intent was to send this clear message to my team: Take care of business while I'm gone. Use your best judgment. The only way you can get in trouble is by failing to take care of business.

That eased some of the bureaucratic tension and in turn increased the level of human spirit and ingenuity.

Even if your part of the garden is small, another good way to remove those weeds is by delegation of authority. Look for someone whom you can trust to make decisions, who can determine which kinds of decisions can be mended if the results are poor—as opposed to those decisions that can't be mended—and give them as much of your official power and protection as you can. If you're struggling with the concept of abdicating your power, remember that you're not giving it away; you're sharing it with respected associates.

Every new manager works in a unique environment. Simply remember the negative impacts of rule making and look for opportunities to weed. This will release a proportionate amount of human spirit and ingenuity. Guaranteed.

4

BUILDING YOUR TEAM:
The Power of Acknowledgment

4
BUILDING YOUR TEAM:
The Power of Acknowledgment

There's a lot of human nature in people.
Mark Twain

Let's start with an assertion that managers are not in the business of fixing people. That's a line of work best reserved for psychologists and professionally trained counselors. Over the years I participated in several sessions called Team Building that focused on just that: fixing people. And the results were always, *always* disastrous. There's nothing wrong with a Meyers-Briggs personality profiling process or a learning styles analysis, but I'll never again ask anyone to participate in one under the guise of team building.

And let me confess that I once asked my staff to go with me on a retreat I billed as "Team Topping" where we had a lot of fun filling out a personality profile and deciding who was an ENJT, or an IN…. We shattered the confidence of only one person at that session. And I kicked myself all the way home.

My focus was wrong. It's like trying to build a better mousetrap by first asking everyone how they feel about themselves and their team members, identifying who is shy, who is an extrovert, who has some deep dark secret hiding in the recesses. No sensible person would start a product improvement conversation this way. Yet companies do it all the time.

> **The manager's job is to focus on the context within which people work.**

In reaction to such sessions, I developed a different retreat style and team building process that worked. I eventually came to see why it worked. This tool was focused on work, work planning, and the collective strengths of the team. I came to believe that when it comes to team building, the manager's job is to focus on the context within which people work.

A Different Team Building Tool

The process I came to prefer as a team building exercise is very straightforward, and it's one anyone can adapt to one's own particular work context. I think it can be especially useful to the new manager wanting to build on the strengths of the work group.

Plan a Three-day Retreat

Find a place to take your team for about three days, a place with few phones, TV, or Internet access—away from all the trappings of modern communications—some restful place where you can all take a deep, relaxing breath.

Arrive Early

Arrive a little before lunch so your team can unpack and orient themselves to the facility. Arrange for a family-style lunch, even if you have it catered. The object is to have everyone start spending time together. Allow a little time after lunch for a stroll or a swim, but at precisely 2:30 PM, call them together.

Bring Supplies

Have on hand a number of flip charts, some tape, and magic markers. It's crude, but informality is part of a good team building process. How many flip charts you use depends on the number of people on your team. Give each member a flip chart.

Make Lists

Invite each team member to privately list everything they did for the last six or twelve months, or whatever time period is important to your organization. Make a list of your own activities. I found it works well if people can be off by themselves during this part of the process. Some people have a tough time getting started, so exercise some patience. This may take longer than an hour.

Regroup

Bring the team back together when it feels like everyone is starting to run out of things to add to their individual lists.

Take the Lead

Begin by explaining why you thought each item on your list is important, unless it's self-evident, of course. Then, invite a critique of your list. By doing this, you show where you've been spending your time. (Creating a positive work environment, right?) You'll also discover whether anyone else thinks this is the right way to spend it. Don't be surprised if a few items are added to your list. Busy people sometimes forget just how much they have accomplished in that agreed-upon time period.

ENGAGE THE TEAM

Then ask for volunteers. No one gets a pass on this exercise, but I found that only the most introverted person needed any push to step forward and prove he or she was important to the team and to the organization. In a very open way, each person has a chance to put a brag list together and then share it. Invariably, I found team members voluntarily adding things to the other individual lists, and I found no occasions when people claimed credit for someone else's work.

This is a powerful and important affirmation of each team member's contribution to the welfare of the corporate whole, the member's value to the company, and to the team itself.

This exercise can be a lot of fun. After a few of these sessions, team members began adding personal improvement actions to the list:

- I stopped smoking!
- I lost 15 lbs.
- I ran a marathon.
- I traveled to Alaska.

- I served on the church budget committee.
- I joined Toastmasters.

Why is this significant? Because adults never outgrow the need for show-and-tell, and because positive work environments have positive effects on the rest of our lives.

While the first part of this process should go easily, this next part could be a little more difficult.

CREATE NEW LISTS

Each team member now builds a new list, a list of things not accomplished during the time period you've previously set. Again, you begin. The list you share is open to challenge, but only in terms of whether your lapses or failures were important to the team and to the organization. This is a good chance to separate the "nice-to-do" from the essential.

I once listed my failure to get us new office space, but while my team said it would be nice to have new office space, it wasn't a priority.

Okay. So now you have lists of accomplishments, and lists of tasks not accomplished. The team has done some bragging, some confessing, and some winnowing. The next step is to take the lists and build a plan for the next work period ahead.

Each team member lists three corporate goals and one personal work-related goal for the coming planning period. These are open to challenge and refinement. Sometimes team members will point out that some planned activities and corporate goals don't focus on external customer needs, or that internal customers needs—theirs—are not addressed. Use this feedback to help team members refine and refocus.

Make sure you're doing the right things, not just doing things right.

The result is a team that knows the condition of the enterprise, how well every member is faring, what there is to be tended to, and what the team is going to do, both individually and together, during the next defined work period.

Summarize

Formalize the plan in writing, and you and your team will have a written checklist of progress and a guide to your activities. When in doubt, check your plan.

Are plans subject to change? Of course, but you still have the advantage of having a point of reference from which to make the change.

Finally, when you have your next planning meeting, your team will have a starting point, and the list of things that didn't get done can be compared to those accomplished. Your work planning will become better and better, and so will the team.

5

THE POWER OF THANK YOU:
Positive Reinforcement & Recognition

5
THE POWER OF THANK YOU:
Positive Reinforcement & Recognition

*Positive reinforcement creates a world from which people
are not likely to defect and which they are likely
to defend, promote, and improve.*
B.F. Skinner

As an employee, all I ever wanted from my boss was a clear notion of what I was supposed to accomplish, the freedom to decide how to get it done, an occasional ear, and backing if things got sticky. I was never good at blindly carrying out orders, and I was never a good yes-man. One of my bosses used to shout, "I don't need yes-men! I already have an opinion!"

However, I always appreciated the occasional pat on the back, a promotion when it was time, and a bit of cash now and then.

I endeavored to build a reputation with the quality of my work and my relationships with others, but I continue to remember the acknowledgment and appreciation of my efforts by others.

Rewards Remembered

As a manager, I never gave the notion of positive reinforcement much thought until I was challenged by a friend to see that most reward systems are flawed. Quiet, dependable people are often overlooked, while those in high visibility jobs and those working directly for people with the power to reward are the only ones being recognized. And as those most frequently rewarded and recognized cycle again and again through company awards ceremonies, the cynicism of the others grows until even well-deserved awards have a negative impact. Consequently, what is envisioned as a positive force actually works against the manager who is trying to create a positive work environment.

> **Most reward systems actually work against the manager who is trying to create a positive work environment.**

That realization reminded me of an experience from my teaching days with my senior elective English students. Somehow, a desk from the grade school was moved into my classroom. In the top drawer was a small box of gold stars. To brighten one slow day, I licked one and put it on an exceptionally good paper, and then made a lighthearted presentation. Thereafter, when papers deserved an exceptional grade, these big, gruff students would go to that desk and get a gold star for their papers. What started as a friendly joke turned into a serious system of awards.

That triggered additional memories of my own grade school years. My dear teacher, Agnes Brown, who taught me more in four years of my grade school days than I learned forever after, was very good about drawing a big red "Good" on work assignments. She used gold stars, silver stars, or no stars if that's what we earned. The stars were things to take home and show Mom and Dad.

> **Even internally motivated people need a way to measure their success.**

In high school, good work earned good report cards or school letters for band and athletics. Scholarship earned Honor Society pins, and ultimately a diploma.

Then we went out into "the cold, cruel world," and for years there was no recognition for good work done, except the paycheck.

For some of us, money is only a temporary incentive. My dad owned several businesses over the years, and as he got older and approached retirement, he said the problem with retirement was that you didn't have any more chances to put another mark on the wall, or to "hit a lick," as he put it. What he was saying was that even internally motivated people need a way to externally measure their success.

My friend, Alex Lafollette, who at that time was working as a commercial fisherman, talked about fishing for a share of the catch. I asked him how that worked. On a small boat, the boat gets a share, the skipper gets a share, and the crew gets a share. So if the boat has a good year, everyone has a good year. It struck me then that everyone must have been focused on the same thing—catching fish. Toward that end, everyone was a problem-solver; everyone pitched in.

My managerial position at the time of this walk down memory lane allowed me a degree of freedom to innovate. So I asked the work force for ideas about creating an equitable and effective incentives system. The ideas ranged from non-cash awards to profit sharing, but most enduring was the notion of peer awards.

Peer Awards

Just like on a fishing boat, your peers know when you've been slacking off or when you've been giving it your best. They know the quiet, unsung heroes—the ones you can call for help on a late Saturday night without getting a lot of guff.

Profit sharing probably needs no lengthy explanation. The only thing unique about the system I created for the Ochoco National Forest was to pay each employee a share of the catch—just like on a fishing boat. If you were a full-time employee, you got an equal share of the total savings, shares being calculated by the total dollar amount of those savings divided by the number of employees.

Even here the manager can position the payout to make it meaningful and fun, for what can be more fun than holding an all-company meeting and passing out bonus checks? It always led to rousing applause for each person and lots of friendly side jokes.

In addition to profit sharing, we also established peer awards. On the Ochoco, peer awards took two forms:

1) A cache of small items like coffee cups, lapel pins, travel clocks, and belt buckles that was available to employees as a way of saying thanks to other employees.

2) A small cash award and a certificate that each employee could give to one other employee in the course of the fiscal year. This was the "Groo Award," named after Tyler Groo, the employee who thought of it.

Of all the incentives, the Groo Award was probably the most enduring and the most significant. One of the unsung heroes received ten Groos in the first month. In a sense, employees were saying, "Okay, Management, you didn't recognize this guy, so we're going to." This is still a coveted award on the Ochoco National Forest, and it continues to help the managers create a positive work environment.

Happy vs. Not Unhappy

Studies of motivation discuss hygiene factors and motivational factors. Hygiene factors relate to things such as decent work environments, benefits, salary, and vacation time. The interesting thing about hygiene factors is that they simply keep people from being unhappy. Not being unhappy is not the same as being happy. If all the hygiene issues are met, people are only in a neutral place.

The Power of Motivation

Motivational factors are a different set. They include such things as personal growth, challenge, a sense of doing significant work, and recognition. If these factors are met, people are motivated, sometimes even when the hygiene factors are not met.

The best examples of this I know are the Incident Management Teams who manage natural disasters such as wildfires, floods, earthquakes, and hurricanes. The hours are long, working conditions are often dangerous and dirty, and sleep may be a catnap after a hurried sandwich and a cup of cold coffee. But anyone who ever served on an Incident Management Team is motivated by mission, challenge, and self worth.

So how does the new manager bring this power to the everyday workplace?

Practice Frequent Recognition

Always thank each individual for good work. Take time to write thank you notes. Use frequent non-cash awards. When deserved, they are valued, and people like to display visible evidence of their success. (Remember those gold stars?)

No adult ever outgrows show-and-tell. We do it all the time. When we get a new vehicle, it's common practice to show it to our friends and then tell them about it. If our kids get their names or pictures in the newspaper, we get copies to share with family and friends.

We're no different in the workplace. We have "I love me" walls with plaques, certificates, pictures, and other objects of accomplishments. We display charts of work in progress, fill bookcases with books we haven't read yet but intend to, all in order to show our value to the company. Coffee cups with company or supplier logos are always in plain sight. This seems to be universal behavior whether we're janitors, receptionists, engineers, or vice presidents.

THE POWER OF THANK YOU

If the manager can use the idea of frequent recognition and positive reinforcement with integrity and honesty, the company benefits, the workers benefit, and families benefit. To paraphrase Tom Peters again, find people doing something right. Remember "Management By Wandering Around"? Finding people doing something right is one payoff of doing this.

Train, Train, Train

Training leads to personal growth and better performance. When you invest time and resources in training your team, you send a message that employees are important. Then you can look for challenging opportunities for people to apply their new skills.

Brag

Publicly brag about your employees. They may squirm a bit in embarrassment, but they like it just the same.

Practice Common Courtesy

Demand common courtesy and practice it. It may not be possible for everyone on your team to like each other, but it is always possible to be courteous. Remember what a sincere "thank you" can do for motivation, morale, and loyalty.

6

ENCOURAGE PARTICIPATION:
Blow the Lid Off That Suggestion Box

6
ENCOURAGE PARTICIPATION:
Blow the Lid Off That Suggestion Box

*I couldn't find the form
to get the form to make the suggestion.*

Properly tended, employee suggestion programs yield tremendous dividends in human spirit and creativity.

Neglected, the employee suggestion process is a sure path to increased employee cynicism and apathy—not exactly a step in the direction of creating a positive work environment.

However, if you're tempted to take a bite from this apple, be sure you're ready to eat it, core and all.

The Locked Box

Recently, I visited an office that contains an employee suggestion box—complete with padlock. I know this box is seldom emptied, and the employees know it's seldom emptied, and so it remains empty. Employees make jokes about the suggestion box, most suggestions run along the line of "Take this box and...." The flow of ideas for improving operations has slowed to a trickle, and employees are back to the old method, getting the boss to make a pitch to the CEO. This means writing more staff papers that go on the stack of all the other staff papers that have yet to be evaluated. Not very exciting stuff. Champions—those people with a passion for the work—have left this company or gone underground.

In an earlier time in this same company, every employee knew that ideas and innovation were highly valued. And they knew ideas could be written on anything—matchbooks, toilet paper, hands, flipcharts, note pads—anything. The form wasn't important. The idea was. It was an exciting, interesting place to work. There was an abundance of champions, and intellectual and physical energies were high. Customers were better served.

> **In those days, response to ideas was immediate.**

In those days, response to ideas was immediate. Sometimes the CEO would look at the idea, regardless of its written form, and approve it on the spot. Sometimes ideas were approved in the hallway. Sometimes volunteer "swat teams" were empowered to dig into the guts of an idea and evaluate its feasibility and ways to implement it. Champions were recognized immediately in team meetings, notices, and informal notes. Sometimes recognition meant some cash, but most people didn't care as long as the idea was adopted.

In one month's time, that organization reviewed and adopted hundreds of new ideas. This led to substantive changes in the way the organization functioned. And three things happened:

- Employees liked working there.
- Customers were new partners in the operation.
- Productivity increased.

It was dynamite! The process, however, was chaotic and tough for the leadership to manage. After all, champions are not easy people to work with. They're often single minded, passionate, very insistent, and sometimes even wrong.

It was like managing a dozen dynamic companies at the same time, armed only with the question "Is it reasoned and reasonable?"

> **It was like managing a dozen dynamic companies.**

After a year or so, the person who insisted on tending to the suggestion process asked for a brief sabbatical, and so another, more systematic thinker shouldered this burden. Unfortunately, he didn't understand the dynamics that were in play, so he created a simple form people could use to make it easier to manage the flow of ideas.

You can guess the rest. The informal approach had worked; this approach didn't. The time it took for someone to write an idea on this "simple" form simply killed a lot of creativity. Brainstorming died a little. Some major ideas floated around now and again, but a lot of people simply stopped contributing their ideas.

When the CEO left the organization, it was the death of the suggestion program. It had been a fun ride, but it was over.

The keys to its original success were recognition of champions, passion for the work of the organization, and speed. There was nothing slipshod about the approach, despite the casual rules about capturing ideas. If the idea looked like it would give added value to the operation, it was given a chance for life. If it failed, it was no big deal; move on to something else, and soon. Under this system, it was common knowledge that if you were willing to share an idea with the CEO you'd better be ready to take it on. Right now. The employees contributed to this process in abundance because they knew their ideas would be respected and considered.

> **They knew their ideas would be respected and considered.**

The locked suggestion box suggests in itself that the company isn't really serious, champions are not welcome, and management knows best after all.

So where does this leave the new manager? Am I saying don't look for new ideas? Not at all. There's just no safe way to do it.

If you do open this Pandora's box, make certain you have the power to act and the energy to manage the chaos that ensues. It can be the most rewarding, challenging time of your working life, and the most demanding. In the eyes of your employees you'll get one of two ratings: pass or fail. Either stay the course, or stay away.

The best work on this subject that I'm aware of is *A Passion for Excellence, The Leadership Difference* by Tom Peters and Nancy Austin.

7

SMOKE & MIRRORS:
The Line-Item Budget

7
SMOKE & MIRRORS: The Line-Item Budget

*Line-item budgets control the money
at the expense of the mission.*

For several years I served on the board of directors of two not-for-profit organizations. In each case, the board was more focused on money than on mission. The amount of money each board managed ranged from a few thousand dollars to around $100,000.

As a forest administrative officer, I also managed budgets for the Ochoco National Forest over a period of almost 16 years. The budgets ranged from $10 million to approximately $26 million.

In spite of the differences in scale, the not-for-profit organizations and the Feds appear to manage their budgets in exactly the same way.

Stages of a Budget

First is the planning stage, always a good step. To arrive at an estimate of what it's going to cost to produce some product or service, it makes good sense to think in increments:
- salary and benefits
- travel
- supplies
- marketing
- communications
- manufacturing
- support services & miscellaneous

Whatever the list, this is a good way to get to a bottom line—lump-sum—number. When we prepare our household budgets, we go through a similar process; we operate with a lump-sum budget. Most organizations, however, depart from the approach we all use in our day-to-day household budgets. While most of us keep our personal money in one checking account, the private and public sector organizations set up many checking accounts, otherwise known as line-item budgets. I don't know of any exceptions to this, including my local church.

> **The private and public sector organizations want to set up many checking accounts.**

The second step in the typical budget process is to allocate an amount of money for each discrete line item. The manager is then accountable for the money in each little pot. And woe to the manager who overspends! The first admonishment I received as a new manager for the Forest Service was, "Don't overspend your budget." Not a word about mission or quality or quantity of work.

Why A Line-Item Budget?

I've puzzled over this question for years, and where I was able, I've challenged the reason for the use of the line-item budget. The answer I received was always the same: for accountability. But the line-item budget is not an accountability tool; it's only a planning tool.

> **Line-item budgeting is managing the money at the expense of the mission.**

The actual allocation of money for an activity or department should be a total dollar allocation, a lump sum to be managed in order to carry out the function or mission of the company or some sub-unit of the organization.

Line-item budgeting is managing the money at the expense of the mission.

Line-item budgets tie the hands of the manager. If the money runs out in a small account, this should terminate the activity linked to that account. It doesn't matter that the manager has a valid mission-based reason to spend additional money on that activity. Even if surplus money is available in another account, the manager winds up managing the money—tracking expenditures and watching the budget—instead of managing the mission. The mission plays second fiddle to the budget. By its very nature, line-item budgets stifle ingenuity and human spirit in a way most lump-sum budgets never do.

It's the function of accountants to track the small costs because that's how the bills arrive. The manager's job is to track the mission.

Planning vs. Allocation

I'm not opposed to line-item planning, but I am opposed to line-item allocations. Those allocations should be lump sums—total dollars for specific, measurable work that meet a measurable standard.

Here's an example of what I mean. Convinced that the old-line, entrenched bureaucracy of the Forest Service was interfering with the ability of field people to carry out the mission of the Forest Service, the chief, Dale Robertson, designated four National Forest Service units as pilot programs outside the normal bureaucratic system. The Ochoco National Forest, of which I was part, was one of those chosen. We could be as innovative as we wanted as long as we didn't break the law.

The first of two requests we made was to be given the authority to take action and make decisions that had been reserved by upper-level management. That was granted. The second request was to be allowed to create and implement a lump-sum budgeting process. That was also granted.

Before that pilot program was created, money had been allocated as 58 discrete line items. By the time the process was complete, seven sub-units also had their share of the 58 discrete line items to track. (All in the name of "accountability" of course.) The Ochoco was so good at line-item budgeting, eventually 700 discrete accounts were created for us to track! In a good year, it took six

> **We could be as innovative as we wanted as long as we didn't break the law.**

to eight weeks to plan and allocate budgets that we hoped would match the mission of the Forest Service.

Under the new pilot program, the budgeting process took six to eight days, not weeks. We worked with only six "checking accounts" (compared to those 700) and paid for a wide range of activities that we had all agreed would support the mission of the Ochoco. This proved to be very cost effective.

In time, the pilot programs became very efficient and mission driven. Unfortunately, because we weren't spending as we had under the line-item system, the mid-level managers outside of these pilot programs cut our budget a whopping 17%.

What's the Lesson?

The lesson appeared to be "use it or lose it." In spite of the budget cuts—or because of them, perhaps—the Ochoco National Forest still met or exceeded all our targets at or above specific standards, and we increased total productivity by 25%. In the second year, productivity increased by 35%. A sister unit, the Mark Twain National Forest in Missouri, had similar results.

A budget cut isn't the measure of the success or failure of any program. You can survive a budget cut if you stay focused on your organization's mission and you have the flexibility to spend money on those high priority targets.

Because line-item budgets are wrapped in the sacred cloak of accountability, line-item budgets stifle the ability of the manager to focus on the mission. Essentially, the budget is in control.

What Do I Do When I Get There?

Budget planning may be made easier by using a line-item approach, but allocations should be made as lump sums. Accountability comes from measuring output, not input. Did the work support the mission of the organization?

When the General Accounting Office decided to pay a visit to the Ochoco, we welcomed them with open arms. And they liked what we were doing. As one auditor put it, "Your accounting system has always been smoke and mirrors. When an organization zeros out all of its accounts, it's working the budget, not doing the work. This is real-world stuff." They understood that it made sense to measure the output—end-results, not the input—money.

The line-item allocation gives incompetent managers a safety net. They can always point to the budget as the flaw, the barrier to getting work done. "If only I had more money..."

> **Accountability comes from measuring output, not input.**

Apart from stifling creativity, line-item budgets make us liars. If there is a surplus, we can count on a reduction in that line item next year, so we always spend the money regardless of the need or its effect on the mission.

This was what the auditors from the GAO were saying—smoke and mirrors.

When I served on Vice President Gore's task force to reinvent government, his National Performance Review, I heard from people from both the private and the public sectors who echoed my experience on the Ochoco National Forest. Their tales reinforced my belief that results-oriented budgeting is the better way.

More importantly, as a member of that task force, I also heard stories about organizations that had changed their budget planning system and the way they tracked accountability. A good book that devotes a fair amount of space to this subject is *Reinventing Government* by David Osborne and Ted Gaebler.

Influencing the Process

What does all this mean for the new manager? First, look at the way your organization plans its budget, and the way it allocates money. These can tell you a great deal about how much flexibility you have to put your share of the money to work. They can also tell you how the organization measures its—and ultimately your—success. Second, if the organization does work the budget instead of the mission, change what you can within the scope of your new position. At the very least, insist on being judged by outcomes, not input.

8

THE DIFFICULT TASK OF FIRING:
With Humanity & Justice For All

8
THE DIFFICULT TASK OF FIRING:
With Humanity & Justice For All

---

*There is enough injustice in this world
without creating any of our own.*

What I liked best about being a manager was the "hero" stuff: hiring, mentoring, promoting, and rewarding deserving people. It's fun to watch a person's face light up when you offer the job. But, like all managers, I also discovered early on that I couldn't duck the hard things even though I wanted to. After all, what adult enjoys disciplining another adult? Or announcing that her job is being eliminated, or he needs to tend to his personal hygiene...and here's a bar of soap. Or his drinking problem is affecting his work and he needs to seek help or be terminated, or she is being terminated during her probationary period because her skills don't suit this kind of work. Or his child was just killed fighting a forest fire.

Those are hard, jagged times.

There are, however, some skills the new manager can develop to handle the tough situations directly, quickly, humanely, and justly.

Inconsistent Work Attendance

The first person I fired didn't work directly for me, but my boss ordered me to handle it—a case of inconsistent work attendance. So I began the business of documenting the facts. Next, I counseled this person, informing her that she had thirty days in which to bring her performance up to expected standards.

> **Rehearse what you're going to say.**

"Here are the standards, here's the documentation of your attendance, here's a letter giving you thirty days to bring your performance up to these standards, and I'll help you if I can." It was time consuming, and it was emotional for her.

At the end of thirty days, she was still having a hard time getting to work on a regular basis, and she wasn't getting anything accomplished when she got there. Then came the next difficult step—delivering the letter terminating her employment. Naturally, this again was a highly-charged situation, and while it was clear that she had to be fired, it was one of the most difficult situations I had to manage. I took away two hard-earned lessons from this experience: When you counsel, rehearse what you're going to say, and stay focused only on the behavior in question.

THE DIFFICULT TASK OF FIRING

After she left, one employee dropped by to see me to say, "I wondered how long you were going to put up with that crap." In failing to counsel this reluctant worker, I hadn't realized what a negative effect she had been on the rest of the work force. The situation certainly hadn't helped create a positive work environment, but sadly, her termination did.

The Chronic Latecomer

Another interesting case was the chronic latecomer. He simply had trouble getting to work on time, but once there, his work was outstanding. After counseling this employee, it occurred to me that I had to decide if it mattered that he was late, and I decided that it didn't matter to me. Nothing had fallen off the end of an assembly line because he wasn't on time. But his being late mattered to his co-workers. It violated their sense of duty, their values. This employee's chronic tardiness was perceived as disrespectful. That he stayed late to make up his work was a justly earned punishment, not a virtue.

To settle the matter, I finally adjusted the employee's schedule to better fit his internal clock. And this was at a time before flexible schedules were in vogue for office workers. Then, I talked with his co-workers individually, and was surprised to discover that as long as he met a set schedule, each of his co-workers was okay. He wasn't late anymore.

> **I had to decide if it mattered that he was late.**

The Vacationer

In another situation, a fellow with a good work reputation began taking lots of unscheduled vacation time, and it was impacting co-workers who had to pick up some of his work in addition to their own. In private, I told the employee, "I value your work, you have an excellent work reputation, but we can't have you gone so much." The employee said, "My spouse is working a graveyard shift so we never get any time together unless I take time off during the day."

> **It was impacting co-workers who had to pick up his work in addition to doing their own.**

So we agreed that the employee would work half-days. This would have to be voluntary according to the rules of the organization and his union contract. I would fill the other half of that position with a second person. This was a simple solution, not very original, but one that worked well for everyone. Production from the two half-time employees was more than we were getting from one full-time person. It had a positive impact on the employee and the work force.

Lost in the Woods

A young man came to work as a junior forester straight from graduate school. He had a bachelor's degree in forestry, and a master's degree in mathematics with emphasis on computer modeling, but he had trouble working in the woods. He had no sense of direction, and he actually got lost, even following a flag

THE DIFFICULT TASK OF FIRING

line. In the office, however, he was a computer whiz. Plus, he was a nice guy.

His manager, also a forester, refused to believe he couldn't do the fieldwork, and waited until the last month of the probationary period to terminate this employee. To make matters worse, the manager had to become angry in order to screw up his courage to confront this unpleasant situation. Some destructive and very unkind things were said, none of which were necessary. The employee was still a very nice person and a willing worker. He was just very inept when it came to fieldwork.

I finally intervened and asked the employee to visit with me. We talked for a bit, then he said, "Mr. Collins, I think those people are mad at me." I suggested they were just frustrated because they wouldn't believe he couldn't do the fieldwork. He was a graduate forester after all, one of them. They believed that he must know how to do the fieldwork but just wouldn't apply himself.

Then he asked, "Am I going to lose my job?" My heart just sank. I finally told him, "Yes." And then we did some career counseling, which should have taken place months before. Together we decided that even though he was very bright, he just wasn't suited to fieldwork, mainly because

> **They wouldn't believe he couldn't do the fieldwork.**

he had no sense of direction and kept getting lost. I made sure he understood this was no reflection on his character or his worth as a person. Together we determined that he was superior in computer modeling of the growth rates of timber stands.

He finally said, "Would it be okay if I just resigned?" I was most grateful for that, and I told him I would do my best to find him a job that suited his talents. He said that would be okay, but he thought that he might already have a job lined up as a computer forester for a large timber company. He had known all along that the situation wasn't working out. He just hadn't known any honorable way out.

Then he thanked me.

For the next couple of years he stopped to visit when his work brought him near my office. He was successful, and had reason to be proud in his new career. And we were friends, not enemies.

I learned another important lesson: Look for creative solutions. You don't have to destroy a person's dignity and pride just because you have to fire them.

The Misfit

Over the years I had several occasions to apply that lesson. In one case, a newly transferred employee didn't seem very happy with his work. In fact he couldn't seem to finish any of the work he was assigned. I finally asked if he really liked his job. He said, "I just hate it."

I remember saying, "What are we going to do now?" He offered to resign effective in six weeks. He also promised to work as hard and diligently as he could to do the work during that time. It wasn't hard for me to agree.

On the other hand, it's much more difficult to deal with people accused of misconduct—stealing, sexual harassment,

THE DIFFICULT TASK OF FIRING

destruction of property, assault, etc. In these cases, and regardless of your personal antipathy for that person or their deeds, you still must deal with the situation justly and make certain to investigate the facts and legalities before proposing termination.

Administrative terminations must presume innocence until proven guilty, and even those guilty of misconduct are entitled to a fair and impartial review.

Another situation a manager may face is work force reduction. I won't dwell on the pain of telling someone the job they've been doing has been eliminated. It's a terrible blow. The message says two things: 1) you're losing your income, and 2) you no longer have value to the company.

> **Administrative terminations must presume innocence until proven guilty.**

The best you can do is have a private meeting, be direct, know what benefits the employee has coming, make sure this information is received in writing, and offer placement assistance. It doesn't really help for you to say how much you value the employee and the work they've done, because they're still digesting messages #1 and #2. I always said it anyway; it made *me* feel better.

Years ago, I realized it made my boss feel better when he told me how much he valued my work, but I was being "downsized" anyway, so I know something of what people feel when they're on the receiving end of this conversation. "Downsized"—what a word! It means, "We ain't mad, but you lose your job anyway."

If your company offers training in supervision, take advantage of this. Go. You might not learn anything new, but a good share of the training will focus on disciplinary actions. Terminating an employee could be avoided with judicious use of job training and job counseling if these are indicated. This is the humane way to proceed. Sometimes a person is simply in the wrong field of work and needs redirection.

> **Sign up for supervisory training.**

If your company doesn't offer training in supervision, your local university or community college probably does. Sign up for supervisory training even if you have to pay for the class out of your own pocket. Trust me; it will save you lots of heartache.

And finally, practice being brave. Even though you may be discomfited, you must have the courage to talk to your employees. If you're uneasy with the business of counseling employees about unwanted behavior, practice what you're going to say. Focus on behavior. Do your best to anticipate the employee's reaction. If you're still uneasy, talk to another manager who seems to know how to do this. Your human resources department is there to help as well.

But counsel you must, because what's often at stake is the employee's economic welfare, the company's welfare, and the health of the work environment—that positive work environment you're working to build and protect.

9

VALUES-BASED NEGOTIATION:
Bargaining Is No Bargain

9
VALUES-BASED NEGOTIATION:
Bargaining Is No Bargain

*Every negotiator has two kinds of interest:
In the substance and in the relationship.*

Roger Fisher and William Ury

There's an additional skill the new manager will want to develop early and perfect over time—the skill of negotiating. Most of us learn our skills by trial and error. Even then, it's often difficult to extract the principles that made the last negotiation successful. Why did this work? Did they just give in? Did I just give in? Was it really about winning and losing? Does compromise mean some losing and some winning? Is negotiating really about compromise?

Winning is a strong American value. What we practice and understand is positional bargaining. What we don't understand is that bargaining is not negotiating

Look at the phrases we use in our everyday transactions:

That's too much.

This is all I will pay.

Will you take *x* for this?

I'm only willing to go this far.

I'll meet you halfway on this.

Take it or leave it.

Do it my way this time, and I'll do it your way next time.

Bargaining is the typical approach we use when we buy vehicles. We bargain, then we judge success by how much we got the dealer to come down in price. Without saying so, it's about winning and losing, and if we think we really put one over on the dealer, we brag to our family and friends to show what great negotiators we are. This is a game the auto sales people usually win, which is why they rank lowest in trustworthy occupations (Morgan Poll, 2002).

The Effects of Positional Bargaining in the Workplace

In the workplace, however, the focus needs to be on building relationships, working toward common goals, creating a positive work environment, building teams, and increasing productivity. Negotiations conducted as positional bargaining always create winners and losers.

Unfortunately, most of corporate America navigates using positional bargaining. The crudest example, and not all that uncommon, is the boss saying, "Do it my way or hit the highway." The boss has the stronger position and you lose. This isn't a good way to bring out the best in people.

The more subtle approach to win-lose lies in citing company policy or tradition, and using it as an amoral cudgel to beat down the opposition. This is sometimes softened with, "I'm really sorry, but that's just the way it is."

The principle is still the same. It's positional bargaining, the success of which is determined by the winner. Before I finally grasped the dynamics of positional bargaining, I remembered leaving one of these "negotiations" with some people who were so kind and understanding that I couldn't be angry. They were sweet about it, but I had been whipped.

I don't like either style much, but if I had to choose, I'd pick the boss who is open about who has the power over the one with the sugar-coated approach.

Another common approach in positional bargaining is to attack the people who oppose your own position. It doesn't take a genius to understand how much lasting damage is done this way; just watch the nightly news. In the workplace, this kind of positional bargaining leads to name calling, recriminations, and revenge, all of which are detrimental to the mission of the organization.

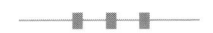

True Negotiating

Fortunately, there are ways to actually negotiate rather than bargain. A very good book on the subject is *Getting to Yes: Negotiating Agreement Without Giving In* by Roger Fish, William Ury and Bruce Patton. Read it. And practice, practice, practice.

Values-Based Negotiations

For my own use, I developed what I call Values-Based Negotiations. I freely admit that anything in Values-Based Negotiations can be found in *Getting to Yes*. I just found it more useful and practical to put the lessons and principles I found in this book into my own frame of reference. I offer this model as a negotiation starter kit to the new manager.

Three words are involved when talking about Values-Based Negotiation:

Principles - Issues - Values

For example, we might all agree to the **principle** of equal pay for equal work. This only becomes an **issue** when people feel the principle isn't being applied to them. Then, the **value** of equity and fair play is in question.

KEEP IT SIMPLE

Keep the process simple and simply focus on principles, issues, and values, not on positions or people. Keeping the communication focused on these three things will permit all parties to work to a common agreement. Values-based negotiating avoids the problems associated with positional bargaining—winning and losing—and it helps the partners reach principled agreements that are understandable and defensible.

COMMUNICATE

Practice good communication skills. For the negotiators, good communication skills mean being able to listen, clarify, and give

VALUES-BASED NEGOTIATION

feedback until all the partners are satisfied that there is common understanding of what's being said. Every partner is entitled to present an issue, to be heard, and to be understood.

Focus on Principles

Keep the communication focused on principles. Watch for words that focus on values. Words like *protection, risk, tradition, security, control, participation,* and *order*. Capture those values the partners agree on. Use those as the focus of discussion.

Record Your Agreement

Always record the agreement that grows from negotiation. Give everyone a written copy and give everyone a chance to wordsmith the draft—with emphasis on *draft*. It isn't an agreement until everyone agrees on the wording, no matter how much you want it to be.

Celebrate Success

Celebrate the process and that the parties worked in unison. Emphasize that *we* all won.

Keep the Agreement Visible

And finally, if misunderstandings arise and disagreements occur, go back to the agreement for clarification. If circumstances have changed to the point that more work is needed, you already have a framework from which to start.

I once was assigned the task of negotiating a new union contract. It started as a typical positional bargaining meeting—union reps on one side of the table, management reps on the other. Tempers were high and positions were absolute. All standard stuff. Positional bargaining requires that you demand more than you really want. Then the compromise winds up in a softer place, and someone still wins. But someone still loses.

Using Values-Based Negotiation, the management team asked only one question: What were the union reps most interested in? It took some work for all of us to move from our starting positions and begin talking.

> **It took some work for all of us to move from our starting position and begin talking.**

The union began talking about the things they really valued: protection of union members from arbitrary actions and/or layoffs, safe working conditions and training, and promotion based on seniority.

We shared their concern for the work force, then we all worked towards some common agreement on each of the issues.

REVIEW THE FACTS

Since there was already a procedure in place to avoid arbitrary disciplinary actions, the only real question to answer together was did it work or did the procedure need tweaking?

On the issue of promotion based on seniority, we looked at the history of promotions under the organization's merit promotion plan. We could all agree that most promotions went to people who had seniority because they had more opportunity and time to train and hone their skills. Those who weren't chosen over junior employees were not considered top performers. Based on the value of doing what's best for the company, the union was satisfied as long as they had representation on the selection panel. That was an easy agreement for all of us.

While the specifics of that agreement with union reps aren't important, the process by which we arrived at agreement is. By identifying our respective values and then working in concert to plan ways to meet those values, we had a very successful negotiation—not positional bargaining. The relationship between the union local and management improved to the point that we were able to work in partnership. This partnership benefited the work force, and it benefited the organization. Because there were only winners in this negotiation, we became stronger and more united.

> **We became stronger and more united.**

One caution: You will not always have reasonable people to work with. I can only recommend that you persevere with the Values-Based Negotiation model and try to keep the focus of your negotiations on principles, issues, and values. If you're unable to be successful using this approach with intractable parties, then at least do your best to be fair.

10

YOUR PROFESSIONAL DEVELOPMENT:
Beyond the Simple Guide

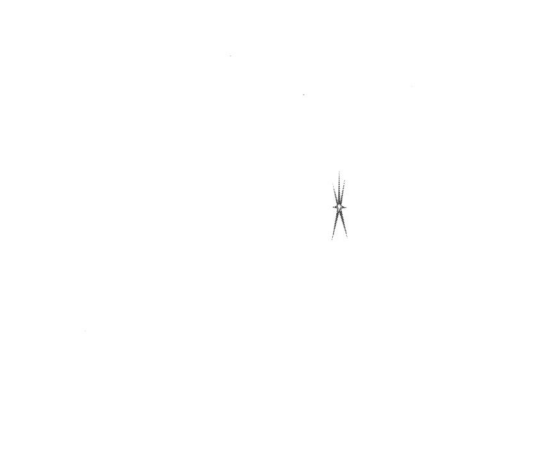

10
YOUR PROFESSIONAL DEVELOPMENT:
Beyond the Simple Guide

---

*The best effect of any book is that
it excites its reader to self actiivity.*
Thomas Carlyle

As a new manager, there is no better investment you can make than in your own education on your own time. Bookstores are packed with good business reads. Some are philosophic, but many are written from a basic how-to approach. Here are some of my favorites:

The Seven-Day Weekend
Ricardo Semler
Portfolio, 2004
This wonderful book is a must-read for all managers, not just new managers. Ricardo Semler writes of his adventures bringing the very simple but extremely complicated and risky concept of democracy to the workplace, in this case in his own companies. He talks of courage, risk, and bringing out the best in people. He also asks some poignant questions, but none that grabbed me more than, "Never mind the cheese! Who moved my weekend?"

In Search of Excellence
Thomas J. Peters and Robert H. Waterman, Jr.
Warner Books, 1982

What most captured my imagination was the focus of the book. Peters and Waterman searched for the best companies they could find in America. Played against the backdrop of the early 1980s and the surging Japanese dominance of world markets, especially in the automotive industry, this book is heady stuff. Much of the management literature written before this book focuses on losers and how they had done it wrong. I'm convinced this book started, or certainly encouraged, the revolution in management leadership in America that helped us regain our preeminent economic position.

The One-Minute Manager
Kenneth Blanchard, Ph.D. and Spencer Johnson, M.D.
Berkley, 1984

The primary lesson in the book is to take time to listen. Since we managers no longer produce those widgets, the best way for us to add value to the company is to listen to those who produce its products and services. We have no other product or service to offer except our brain and our time.

ZAP! The Lightning of Empowerment:
How to Improve, Productivity, and Employee Satisfaction
William C. Byham
DDI Press, 1989

The book focuses on the basic principles "of empowering people, about helping employees take ownership of their jobs so they take personal interest in improving the performance of the organization." I've given away dozens of copies of this book to subordinates, friends, and peers.

Bringing Out the Best in People
Aubrey C. Daniel
McGraw-Hill, 1994

I liked this book before I ever read it. I was impressed by the thoughtfulness of the title. It wasn't focused on the exploitation of people, but on the power of positive reinforcement. After that, I was as delighted with the contents of the book as I was with the title. Daniels' Golden Rule: "When positive reinforcement becomes a way of life in the organization, with reinforcement going from boss to subordinate, peer to peer, and peer to boss, adversarial relationships begin to disappear. People begin to treat each other as they would like to be treated."

A Journey Into the Heroic Environment
Rob LeBow
Prima, 1997

This is a powerful, practical book that every new manager should read. Based on 17 million surveys from 40 countries about what employees really want and need to be successful in their work lives, Lebow's "Eight Principles of the Heroic Environment" have application beyond our corporate working lives. It's as much about living a "heroic life" as it is about working.

Joy at Work: A Revolutionary Approach to Fun on the Job
Dennis W. Bakke
PVG, 2005

A summary of Bakke's philosophy is no more complicated than the motto of Dr. James Mayo, founder of the famous medical clinic: "There is no fun like work." The key to joy at work is the personal freedom to take actions and make decision using individual skills and talents.

Beyond the Bottom Line
Martin W. Sandler and Debra A. Hudson
Oxford University Press, 1998
   This book is full of detailed stories of non-profit and government agencies "that are meeting the challenge of doing more with less, and setting standards of efficiency and service that few business organizations can meet." The appeal of this book lies in stories of ordinary Americans accomplishing extraordinary things in a public sector environment.

Reinventing Government
David Osborne and Ted Gaebler
Plume, 1993
   This is another good book for those in a public sector career.

Leaders
Warren Bennis and Burt Nanus
Harper and Row, 1985
   If nothing else, this book will give you insight into the dilemmas of trying to study and learn leadership.

A Passion for Excellence
Tom Peters and Nancy Austin
Random House, 1985
   If you read nothing else in this excellent book, read Chapter 10, Three Skunks. I also found the introduction especially compelling. Peters and Austin say, "...we advocate a change from 'tough-mindedness' to 'tenderness,' from concern with hard data and balance sheets to concern for the 'soft stuff'—values, vision and integrity…"

BEYOND THE SIMPLE GUIDE

Getting to Yes: Negotiating Agreement Without Giving In
Roger Fisher, William Ury and Bruce Patton
Penguin Books, 1991
    I firmly believe that reading and studying this book improved my negotiation skills, not only in the workplace, but in my personal life as well.

    What, no mention of W. Edward Deming? Yes. Read Deming, too. The Japanese did.

    I know there are dozens of books that can be added to this list, but these are some that I felt would be the most immediately practical for the new manager.

    Your community college will have workshops or distance learning centers that will be of value. Read the trade magazines related to your field, and if there are professional societies that you are eligible to join, do that too.

    And finally, enjoy the journey.

11

CHAPTER SUMMARIES:
The Shortcut

11
CHAPTER SUMMARIES:
The Shortcut

1 FIRST DAYS: Walk, Look, & Listen

- Focus on the right things.
- Manage by wandering around.
- Learn the routine business of your staff.
- Listen, listen, listen.
- Stress honesty.
- Give credit where credit is due.
- Create a positive work environment.

2 LEADERSHIP: It's All Around You

- Leaders have followers.
- The Great Myth: Leaders occupy the top positions in organizations.
- Fact: Leaders work at all levels of organizations.

- A good manager provides opportunities for leaders at all levels to bring their skills to the workplace.
- The primary job of the manager is to create a positive work environment.
- Emergency situations may require the exercise of power.
- True power lies in direct correlation to responsibility.

3 RULES & REGS:
Weed Your Bureaucratic Garden

- The most important ingredient in business success is human spirit and ingenuity.
- Common sense structure is needed for successful human enterprise.
- Unnecessary structure stifles human spirit and ingenuity.
- Untended structure grows and will put an organization in crisis.
- Make no unnecessary rules.
- Weed your part of the bureaucratic garden.

4 BUILDING YOUR TEAM:
The Power of Acknowledgment

- Managers are not in the business of fixing people.
- Managers are in the business of fixing the context within which people work.
- Team building should focus on work and the workplace, not on personalities.
- Adults never outgrow "show-and-tell."

THE SHORTCUT

- Positive work environments have positive effects on the rest of our lives.
- Make sure you are doing the right things, not just doing things right.

5 THE POWER OF THANK YOU
Positive Reinforcement & Recognition

- Practice frequent recognition.
- Remember your unsung heroes.
- The simplest form of positive reinforcement is common courtesy.
- Train, train, train. Training says "I think you are important."
- Demand courtesy and practice it.

6 ENCOURAGE PARTICIPATION:
Blow the Lid Off That Suggestion Box

- Properly managed suggestion programs yield tremendous dividends in human spirit and creativity.
- The ingredients of a useful suggestion program are: Recognition of Champions • Passion • Speed
- Dynamic suggestion processes are chaotic and essentially "skunk works" in nature.
- There is no safe way to do it.
- Stay the course or stay away.

7 SMOKE & MIRRORS: The Line-Item Budget

- Line-item planning is a good tool.
- Line-item budgeting is managing the money at the expense of the mission.
- Line-item budgets stifle ingenuity and human spirit.
- Allocations should be lump sums—total dollars for specific, measurable work to measurable standards.
- Accountability comes from measuring work output, not budget input.
- Line-item budgets make us liars. We spend the surplus to protect our share of next year's budget.
- Insist on being judged by outcomes, not input.
- Change what you can.

8 THE DIFFICULT TASK OF FIRING: With Humanity & Justice For All

- Counsel early and frequently with performance problems.
- Always counsel in private, and focus on behavior.
- Document the counseling.
- Base counseling on established performance standards.
- Provide help and a reasonable opportunity for improvement.
- Look for creative solutions. (Deals can be okay.)

- Fire people when they deserve to be fired, but don't destroy their humanity, or yours, in the process.
- Take a class in supervision.
- Be brave, or at least act that way.

9 VALUES-BASED NEGOTIATION
Bargaining Is No Bargain

- Positional bargaining is about winning and losing.
- Value-Based Negotiation depends on finding common values from which to build agreement.
- Practice good communication skills. Listen, clarify and give feedback until all parties have a common understanding of the issues and values at stake.
- Make sure that all parties have a voice in the negotiations.
- Focus on principles and values, but not on positions or people.
- Record all agreements in writing.
- Celebrate successful negotiations.

Acknowledgments

Some years back I wrote a letter to each of the people who helped a callow youth along the way. Sometimes the help was a summer job, sometimes it was a kick in the rear at a critical time, sometimes it was simple encouragement and advice. Almost all of those who helped me grow from child to adult have reached the end of life. The only person I didn't thank in time was Agnes Brown, my grade school teacher, who paddled me, pushed me and loved me in ways I didn't understand until I was in my mid-thirties.

Vi Collins, my bright companion, friend, and wise critic; John Collins, friend and teacher until his death at age eighty-three; Wanda Collins, whose humor and strength carried us through the hard times; Dean Collins, who taught me to lead with my left.

Professor Robert Baker, who flunked me on a mid-term because "You are getting lazy, Rod"; Doctor Jack Bellamy, whose sense of humor and high standards kept me going back for more; Wright Mallory, Forest Supervisor, Mt. Hood National Forest; F. Dale Robertson, Chief, USDA Forest Service, retired—Thanks for your faith in me. Dave Rittersbacher, Forest Supervisor, Ochoco National Forest, a great leader; J.C. Hansen, a good friend and one of the best minds in the U.S. Forest Service; Bill Delaney, who kept at me to push the envelope, and who always covered my back; Alex Lafollette, a true Renaissance man; Eva Long, editor extraordinaire; Shelley Blumberg, enthusiastic proofreader; Julia O'Reilly, a truly creative artist; Dale Casey, friend and critic.

Thank you, all.

ROD COLLINS lives with his wife, Vi, in Springfield, Oregon, in the foothills of the Cascade Mountains. Six children and eleven grandchildren call it safe harbor.

Rod retired from the Forest Service in 1999, and is now an author, publisher, and management consultant.

In addition to *What Do I Do When I Get There? A New Manager's Guidebook*, Rod is the author of a novel, *Spider Silk*, published by Publishamerica.com.

Please direct inquiries regarding speaking, seminars, and consulting to *rod@brightworkspress.com*.

Notes

Quick Order Form

For additional copies of this book

	Qty	Price	Total
What Do I Do When I Get There?		@ $15.95 each	
Subtotal			

Discounts

For 5 or more books, subtract 5% off cover price

For 10 or more books, subtract 10% off cover price

Shipping & Handling

Add $2.95 for each book

TOTAL AMOUNT

Ship to:

Name _____

Address _____

City _____

State/Zip _____

Phone _____

Email _____

I understand that I may return any order for a full refund, no questions asked.

Make checks payable to: **Bright Works Press**

Mail to:
Bright Works Press
36597 Alder Branch Road, Springfield, OR 97478